A Glut
of
Apricots
&
Peaches

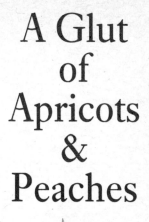

Ann Carr

Illustrated by
Martin MacKeown

MEREHURST PRESS
—— LONDON ——

*The Publishers wish to thank
Rosemary Wilkinson and Malcolm Saunders
for their help with this book.*

First published 1988 by Merehurst Press
5 Great James Street
London WC1N 3DA

Produced by
Malcolm Saunders Publishing Ltd
26 Ornan Road, London NW3 4QB

Copyright © 1988 this edition
Malcolm Saunders Publishing Ltd
Copyright © 1988 text Ann Carr
Copyright © 1988 design
and illustrations Martin MacKeown

All rights reserved. No part of this publication may be
reproduced, stored in a retrieval system, or transmitted
in any form or by any means, electronic, mechanical,
photocopying, recording, or otherwise, without the
prior written permission of the copyright owners.

ISBN 0 948075 99 6

Photoset in Linotype Ehrhardt
by Fakenham Photosetting Limited
Printed in Spain

CONTENTS

FOREWORD

Oh for a complexion of peaches and cream or an apricot blush of summer! So thought many a young girl a century ago and, I suspect, so does the modern miss, if she would but admit it.

And how right the saying is, for peaches and cream are not only exquisite to eat but also, together in a bowl, display the softest and subtlest shades of colour, while a ripe apricot in high summer has a glow like a lighted candle. It is unlikely, though, that any girl would long for a complexion like that of the nectarine with its rosy, dark skin. It is not only the lovely colours and soft bloom that link the peach and the apricot with the complexion of a young girl; the stone in the centre of the peach contains a kernel, the oil from which has been used in cosmetic preparations for hundreds of years.

These fruits, once so rare outside their country of origin, are now exported in great quantities from early spring till late autumn. There are exquisite small white peaches of the sweetest and subtlest flavour, huge yellow peaches, little firm nectarines, red almost all over, larger nectarines, yellow and dark, plush-red, and there are free-stone or slipstone peaches and cling-stone peaches. Apricots have a shorter season but they, too, come in

varying shades and sizes, some with a pink blush and some without.

These fruits have added much to our summer eating and, with their warm colours, subtle flavours and natural sweetness, complement the slightly astringent sharpness of soft fruits, such as red and white currants, raspberries and strawberries.

Apricots and peaches need a really warm summer to produce real depth and strength of flavour, though less perfectly ripened fruit cook well. Local greengrocers and markets will have their own gluts, for these are fragile fruits and must be used quickly. Throughout the season it is possible to buy reasonably cheap apricots and peaches to experiment with in the kitchen at home.

11

INTRODUCTION

The apricot, *prunus armeniaca*, probably came to us from China, where it has been grown for four thousand years, though it is impossible to be sure, for it is grown throughout Asia and the Middle East and is a staple food there.

The apricot tree is hardier than either the peach or the nectarine and does fairly well in temperate climates; the main difficulties in producing a heavy crop are that the trees flower early and the blossoms may be blown away by high winds or late frosts in spring and the fruit may never reach its peak of perfection through lack of summer warmth. An apricot, picked warm and in perfect condition, has a wonderful smell and taste.

Imported apricots are picked unripe and, although their colour may be glowing, the fruit itself often lacks flavour and is hard or dry and spongy.

Spain exports apricots to the rest of Europe; California is said to produce the best apricots for eating fresh; Turkey and Iran for eating dried. Afghanistan produces

Apricot

Apricot

the superb, small, round Hunza apricot, that is dried whole and is quite delectable to eat as it is, or cooked.

A fruit tree of the rose family, *rosaceae*, it is believed the peach originated in China, rather than Persia, the country after which it is named: *prunus persica*. The two main factors pointing to this belief are, firstly, the peach tree grows wild in China and nowhere else in the world and, secondly, it breeds true from seed there, which is not the case anywhere else. These two facts suggest that all other peaches are hybrids. From Persia the peach reached Italy and thence it spread through Europe (Pliny named it the Persian Apple – 'malum persicum'), reaching England via France. Sadly, France has lost its most famous of peaches, the Montreuil; the district where these splendid peaches once grew is now a hideous suburb.

Peach trees grown in the temperate parts of the northern hemisphere need warm, sunny, sheltered corners or a greenhouse if they are to produce flavoursome, juicy fruit. Before modern cold storage and freighting made exporting so much easier, many more peach and apricot trees were grown on the south walls of the garden or house. Now there are imports from Italy, Spain and France, though America is the world's main producer, especially of the yellow cling peach which is used in the canning industry. Canada and Australia are also major producers and canners.

There are many varieties of peach, both white and yellow-fleshed. The white-fleshed

Peach

is considered the finest dessert peach. Unless you grow your own, or have a knowledgeable greengrocer, you are unlikely to
know what type of peach you have bought
until you get it home and start to peel or stone
it. Few sellers are knowledgeable enough to
be able to tell their customers if the peaches
are cling-stone or free-stone (slipstone),
easy peelers or needing the boiling water
treatment. However, you will be able to tell
whether you are buying white or yellow-

17

fleshed fruits: white-fleshed peaches have a pale pink blush and a milky, creamy tinge to their skins. The yellow-fleshed fruits have deep, yellow-to-ochre skins touched with dark pink.

Unfortunately, many of the old varieties of peach that grew in the gardens of Europe and were written about with great relish as to their fine flavour, excellence or beauty, are now lost forever and what we buy in shops and markets are fruits specially bred for travelling.

The peach tree is relatively short-lived and commercial growers may replace as frequently as every eight to ten years. In spite of the short life of the tree itself, the fruits are a

Peach

symbol of longevity and friendship and were often given as tokens to show lasting affection. Not only the fresh fruits were given but exquisite porcelain and silver peaches also were made in China and Persia as tokens to be exchanged. The Chinese believed that peaches eaten before death preserved the body from corruption 'until the end of the world'. Still today in China a round, steamed dumpling filled with peach is made and served on birthdays. The stone itself is often carved into beads and charming boxes.

The kernel of the peach stone, as well as its oil, is sometimes used in cooking. Peach

Nectarine

juice is soothing and can be used as a mild diuretic; firm, fresh peaches, peeled and eaten in small quantities are given to soothe an upset stomach.

The nectarine, *prunus persica nectarina*, is not a separate species, but a smooth-skinned variety of the peach, sometimes called the plum peach, for it is without the peach's fine, velvet coating. However, like the peach, there are white and yellow-fleshed fruits. The texture of the flesh is more variable than that of the peach; some fruits are moist and fibrous, others firm-fleshed but all have a superb flavour, more akin to white than to yellow peaches and, in cooking, retain more flavour and scent than peaches do.

Like the peach, the nectarine has come to us from China via Persia and also like the peach, to grow in the northern hemisphere it requires a warm and sheltered spot. It is, in fact, a more delicate tree than the peach and is probably best grown under glass or only in the warmest corners.

Nectarine

A strange desire I had To eat some fresh Nectaren's.

> *(1676, Sir George Etherege 'The Man of Mode')*

COOKS' NOTES

1. Unless specific details are given in the individual recipes, the following apply:
– spoon measurements are level
– sugar is granulated
– eggs are standard size
2. Follow either the imperial measurements or the metric but do not mix them, as they have been calculated separately.
3. As individual oven temperatures vary, use the timings in the recipes as a guide. Always preheat your oven or grill.

The
Recipes

APRICOTS

Who wants to use the familiar dried fruits if, when there is a glut, the fresh apricots are available at reasonable prices? To eat the sun-warmed fruit straight from the tree is the ideal thing, for the apricot, when fresh, is best eaten at room or garden temperature. Its elusive flavour is lost when it is chilled or stored in the refrigerator. Sadly, much of the imported fruit we buy has suffered from being picked unripe and chilled while it is transported to the markets. Gluts, unless from the garden, are perhaps best turned into tarts, compotes, purées or puddings.

The dried apricot, like yogurt, is full of food value and folk lore but the fresh apricot is not without its virtues, for it is rich in vitamin A and, unlike strawberries and other delicately-flavoured fruits, its taste is enhanced by cooking and blending with other flavours. The kernel in the stone can be eaten and used to give a sharp almond flavour, though only in moderation for, cumulatively, they are poisonous. Despite this, like peach stones, they are much used in France in liqueurs or eaux de vie.

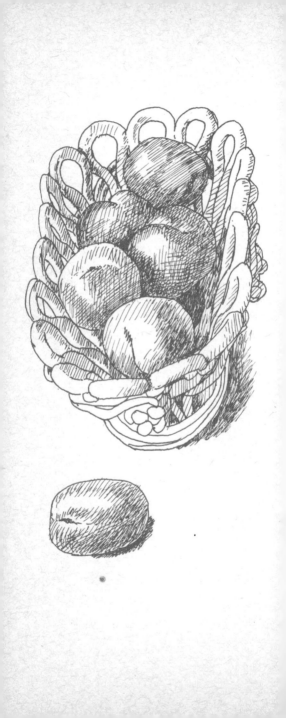

*There be two kindes of peaches ... The other
kindes are soner ripe, wherefore they are called
abrecox or aprecox.*

*(1578, Henry Lyte 'Dodoens' Niewe herball or
historie of plantes')*

Apricots Stuffed with Cream Cheese

This makes a light starter or is good with
summer drinks, or champagne.

Serves 4–6
2–3 apricots per person
4 oz (125 g) curd cheese
2–3 tablespoons milk
1 oz (30 g) toasted almonds, chopped
1 teaspoon chopped chives
2 teaspoons chopped fresh parsley
salt and pepper, to taste
*1 split toasted almond per apricot half, to
decorate*

Wash and halve apricots, removing stones.
Mix together curd cheese and milk in a bowl,
add all the other ingredients except decoration and mix well. Use this mixture to stuff
the apricot halves, top with a split toasted
almond, chill and serve.

Yond dangling Apricocks.
(1593, Shakespeare 'Richard II, Part III, Act
iv, Scene 29')

Chicken Fillets with Fresh Apricots

This fresh apricot relish is particularly good with chicken fillets. Serve with plain boiled new potatoes and a green summer vegetable.

Serves 4
8–10 apricots, depending on size
1 teaspoon very finely chopped onion
1/2 teaspoon chopped fresh mint
1 teaspoon sugar
2–3 teaspoons wine vinegar
salt and pepper, to taste
1 1/2–2 oz (45–60 g) butter
4 chicken breasts

To prepare apricots, blanch and peel, if liked, otherwise wash, dry, cut in half lengthwise and remove the stones, keeping four halves for decoration. Chop remaining apricots into quarters, then eighths; place in a bowl and add onion, mint, sugar, vinegar, salt and pepper. Mix gently and leave to marinate while cooking chicken – or longer if liked – but beware for the fruit may turn brown.

Gently heat butter in a large frying pan, do not allow to brown, add chicken breasts and cook gently for 3 to 4 minutes on each side, depending on thickness of meat. Serve the chicken topped with half an apricot and a teaspoon or more of marinated apricot as an accompaniment.

Apricots with Noisettes of Lamb

This dish is traditionally made with dried apricots but try it with the fresh fruit. As it is an expensive dish, it is worth using only the best loin of lamb available. Noisettes are cut from the loin; the best way to enjoy them is off the bone, the butcher will do this for you and all you need do is slice the meat into ½ inch (1 cm) slices.

Serves 4

1 lb (500 g) apricots

2 oz (60 g) butter

2 teaspoons chopped onion

1 teaspoon garam masala

2 fl oz (60 ml) dry or medium sherry

1 tablespoon chopped fresh mint

salt and pepper, to taste

2–3 noisettes of lamb per person, 4 if very small

1–2 tablespoons cooking oil

a sprig of mint, to decorate, for each serving

To make the sauce, blanch and peel apricots, then purée in a blender or food processor. Melt butter in a saucepan, add onion and garam masala and fry very gently for 5 to 10 minutes, until onion is clear and cooked. Add to apricot purée and whizz until smooth, then return to the saucepan, add sherry,

mint, salt and pepper, mix well and set aside.

To cook the meat, heat oil in a frying pan, add noisettes and quickly fry for 2 minutes on each side – if you like them pink – or longer if liked, remove and keep warm. Skim all the fat from the frying pan and pour in half the apricot purée. Bring almost to boiling point, scraping the bottom of the pan well. Add to purée in saucepan and reheat.

Arrange noisettes on a serving dish, pour a little of the sauce round them, not on or over, and decorate with mint sprigs. Serve remaining sauce separately in a jug or sauce boat.

Pork Hot Pot with Apricots

A pleasant summer casserole.

Serves 6
2 tablespoons cooking oil
1 shallot, chopped
2 carrots, sliced
1½ lb (750 g) lean stewing pork, cubed
3 sprigs thyme
3 sage leaves
10 fl oz (315 ml) light stock
1 lb (500 g) apricots, halved and stoned
8 oz (250 g) fresh green peas
salt and pepper, to taste
2 teaspoons grain mustard

Heat oil in a flameproof casserole with a tight-fitting lid, add shallot and carrots and stir-fry for 4 to 5 minutes, do not brown. Add pork and stir-fry for a further 5 minutes, then stir in herbs, stock and half the apricots. Cover tightly and cook slowly for ¾ to 1 hour, until meat is tender. Uncover, remove herbs and stir in remaining apricots, peas, salt, pepper and mustard. Cover and cook for a further 10 to 15 minutes until peas and apricots are tender.

Apricot
stone

Gammon & Glazed Apricots

Gammon can be very dry, so it helps to brush it with butter or oil during the cooking.

Serves 4
4 thick gammon slices
2 oz (60 g) butter, melted
12 apricots
2 teaspoons sugar
6 fl oz (185 ml) sour cream
1 tablespoon sweet mustard, e.g. German
or Swedish type
1 tablespoon chopped chives

Brush gammon slices with butter, place on a grill pan and grill quickly for 2 minutes on each side, or according to thickness. Remove, place in a hot ovenproof dish and keep warm. Halve apricots, remove stones, sprinkle with sugar and glaze under the grill, then arrange on top of gammon and keep warm. Mix together sour cream, mustard and chives in a bowl, spoon over apricots and gammon, place the dish under the hot grill and grill for 1 to 3 minutes until the sauce bubbles. Serve hot.

Of trees or fruits to be set or remooued; 1 Apple-trees. 2 Apricockes.

(1573, Thomas Tusser 'Fiue hundreth pointes of good husbandrie')

Apricot Cream

This is a soft, velvety cream, rich and delicious. Avoid using vanilla essence; if possible use a pod or pure vanilla extract.

Serves 6
1¹/₂ lb (750 g) apricots
1 oz (30 g) butter
2–4 fl oz (60–125 ml) water
¹/₂ a vanilla pod or ¹/₄ teaspoon vanilla extract
2 egg yolks, beaten
1¹/₂ tablespoons cornflour
10 fl oz (315 ml) creamy milk
6 fl oz (185 ml) double (heavy) cream, whipped

Blanch apricots, peel, halve and stone. Melt butter in a saucepan with a tight-fitting lid,

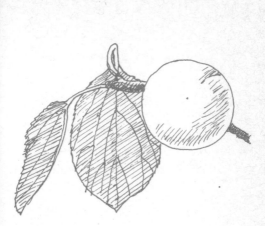

add apricots, water and vanilla pod, if used. Do not, at this stage, add extract or, worse still, essence. Cover tightly and simmer gently for 10 to 15 minutes or until cooked. Watch carefully to see that they do not burn.

When cooked, remove vanilla pod, transfer fruit and liquid to a blender or food processor and purée. Mix together egg yolks and cornflour in a bowl, stir well, add milk and tip all into a saucepan and cook, stirring all the time, over a low heat. As mixture begins to thicken, pour in apricot purée, stirring continuously until cream cooks and thickens, taking care it does not become lumpy. When thick and cooked, add vanilla extract, if using, and pour into a bowl. Leave to cool, stirring occasionally to prevent a skin forming. When quite cold, fold in whipped cream.

Apricot Purée

This is quickly made, keeps for two to three weeks in the fridge and can be used as a sauce or added to cream for ices or fools: 1½–1¾ lb (750–875 g) fruit will make 20 fl oz (625 ml) before any other ingredients are added.

For every 2 lb (1 kg) of apricots, add 10 fl oz (315 ml) white wine and 2 oz (60 g) sugar. You can, at this stage, add a flavouring, such as vanilla or cinnamon, cloves or allspice. Wash the fruit, halve and remove the stones, then place in a saucepan, adding wine, sugar and flavouring – if used. Cover tightly and simmer for 15 to 20 minutes, stirring occasionally. When cooked, purée in a blender or food processor. Bottle in clean jars or plastic containers. Cover and store.

A bead from a necklace of fifty-four individually carved apricot stones, each of half-inch diameter

Apricot

Apricot Cheese

A very quick dessert or tea-time dish for children.

Serves 4
8–10 apricots
8 oz (250 g) curd cheese
1–2 oz (30–60 g) sugar, or to taste
juice of 1 orange
1 teaspoon grated orange peel
mint leaves or chopped fresh mint, to
decorate

Wash fruit, halve and remove stones. Chop roughly, place in a blender or food processor and purée. Add all the other ingredients except the decoration and purée again. Spoon into a serving dish and chill for at least an hour before serving. Sprinkle with mint just before serving.

Apricots with Amaretto

This dish uses fresh apricots in a thickened sauce flavoured with Amaretto liqueur – the fruit itself is not cooked.

Serves 6
2 lb (1 kg) ripe apricots
16–18 fl oz (500–560 ml) white wine
2 tablespoons cornflour
2 fl oz (60 ml) Amaretto (almond) liqueur
2–4 oz (60–125 g) sugar, or to taste

Reserve 6 of the best and ripest fruit for decoration, do not skin. Place remaining apricots in a bowl and pour over boiling water, lift out and skin, halve and remove stones, then place in a flameproof serving dish. Heat wine in a saucepan over a low heat. Mix cornflour and Amaretto together in a small bowl, add a little of the warm wine, then pour all back into the saucepan and stir carefully with a wooden spoon until the mixture thickens and becomes clear. Add sugar, stir until dissolved, then pour over apricots. Mix gently and leave to cool. Decorate with reserved apricots, halved and stones removed.

Abricocts are ready to be eaten in Summer.
(1601, Philemon Holland 'Pliny's Historie of the World')

Hot Rice with Apricots

A most unusual dessert – a sweet pilaf is quite delicious.

Serves 6

14 oz (440 g) rice, long grain, or Italian type rice – not pudding rice

14 fl oz (440 ml) water

14 fl oz (440 ml) white wine

peel and juice of 1 orange

2–3 tablespoons runny honey, or to taste

1 lb (500 g) fresh apricots, halved and stoned

2 oz (60 g) toasted almonds, chopped

Greek-style plain yogurt, to serve

Wash rice and place in a saucepan with a tight-fitting lid, add water, wine and about 1 in (2.5 cm) of the orange peel, bring to the boil, cover, lower heat and leave to simmer undisturbed for 20 to 25 minutes; the rice should only just simmer, until tender. Remove from the heat, discard orange peel and, with a fork, fluff up the cooked rice; all the cooking liquid should be absorbed. Add orange juice, honey and fresh apricots, mix well, cover with a tea towel and the lid, and leave to rest for 5 to 10 minutes.

To serve, turn out onto a warm serving dish, sprinkle with toasted almonds and hand round a dish of yogurt.

Apricot Jelly

This is a very pretty summer dessert. Serve with a raspberry purée for contrast, or an apricot purée, lightly spiced or flavoured with mint.

Serves 6
1½ lb (750 g) apricots
2 oz (60 g) sugar
6–8 fl oz (185–250 ml) water
juice of 1 orange
5 teaspoons powdered gelatine

Halve apricots and remove stones, place in a saucepan with a tight-fitting lid, add sugar, water and orange juice, cover and simmer for 15 to 20 minutes or until tender. Rub through a sieve for a really fine-textured jelly. Place 3–4 tablespoons of the hot purée in a small bowl, sprinkle over gelatine and dissolve over a basin of hot water, then stir into rest of purée. Rinse a 2 pint (1.2 litre) jelly mould in cold water, pour in apricot mixture and leave to set.

To serve, turn out onto a plate and pour round a purée of raspberries or apricots or a thin custard sauce.

Apricot Fool

This can be made with peach or nectarine purée, but the flavour is better using apricots. It will serve 4 to 6 people.

For 20 fl oz (625 ml) thick apricot purée, use 1½ lb (750 g) fresh fruit, halved and stoned, peeled if you like but if using really ripe fruit this is not necessary; sugar to taste – this depends on how good a flavour the fruit has, how ripe and how naturally sweet, 1–2 tablespoons is generally enough; 1 teaspoon grated orange peel; 1–2 tablespoons Amaretto (almond) liqueur or an orange liqueur if you prefer. Cook together over a low heat until tender. Transfer to a blender or food processor and purée. Leave to cool. Whip 6 fl oz (185 ml) double (heavy) or whipping cream, fold in 6 fl oz (185 ml) thick Greek-style plain yogurt, then fold in the apricot purée. Pour into a serving dish and chill well before serving.

Apricot Crumble

The nibbed almonds make this topping deliciously crunchy.

Serves 4
1 lb (500 g) apricots
3 oz (90 g) sugar
4 oz (125 g) plain flour
2 oz (60 g) butter
2 oz (60 g) nibbed almonds

Halve apricots, remove stones and lay them in a baking dish. Sprinkle 1 oz (30 g) of the sugar on top.

To make the crumble, place flour in a bowl, add butter and rub into flour until the mixture looks like fine breadcrumbs. Alternatively, process in a food processor. Add remaining sugar and nibbed almonds, mix well together and spoon over the apricots. Bake at 190 °C (375 °F/Gas 5) for 20 to 25 minutes, until fruit is cooked and top pale golden. Serve hot or warm.

Apricot Conserve

It is often thought that a conserve is merely jam by a grander name but this is not so. Strictly speaking, a conserve is a syrup in which the whole fruit is preserved. I make what I consider to be a conserve but I do halve the fruit to remove the stones, which should really be removed with a sharp knife through the top of the very ripe apricot. Many apricot conserve recipes tell you to remove the skins but I like the additional flavour they give to the finished conserve.

To every 1 lb (500 g) of ripe fruit put 1 lb (500 g) of sugar. Halve the apricots and remove the stones. In a deep bowl place alternate layers of sugar and apricots, cover with a clean tea towel and leave overnight. Next day tip into a preserving pan or large saucepan and very, very slowly, bring to the boil, stirring constantly, then boil until the fruit is clear and the syrup begins to thicken. Do not boil as fast as you would to achieve a set in jam-making. When the syrup is thick and the fruit clear, remove from the heat, leave aside until warm, then pot in sterilized jars, cover and store in a cool, dry place (see page 88). Keeps for 3 to 4 months.

PEACHES

The peach is the perfect fruit for a still life; an arrangement of prime fruits should be on a beautiful pedestal dish waiting to be eaten on a summer day, so ripe that the juice will run down the wrist when the fruit is bitten into. Unless you have a peach tree you are unlikely to find such perfection, though imported fruits are improving and often have a sweet scent and succulent flesh.

Many of these recipes require that the peaches or nectarines be skinned first. Really ripe peaches may skin without blanching, otherwise pour boiling water over them and leave for 15 to 20 seconds – longer if they are rather unripe. If poaching the fruit, add the skins to the liquor and remove when the fruit is cooked, the skins add colour and flavour. The yellow clingstone peaches are most commonly used for cooking but the lovely white-fleshed peaches have by far the better flavour, although the cooked peach halves or slices will not be so perfect-looking and the juice will not be so clear.

When buying peaches, choose carefully, a tray of soft peaches going cheap is not worth even the bargain price asked; the fruit will not even cook well – it will be woolly and worthless. Look for fruit that is unbruised, firm but not hard.

Try peaches and Parma ham, peaches fried in brown sugar and rum, or with a real glut, peach jam.

And many hoomly trees ther were
That peches, coynes, and apples bere.
(1366, Geoffrey Chaucer 'The Romaunt of the
Rose')

Peach Vinaigrette

This is an unusual summer salad and good served as a starter. Allow about three-quarters of a peach per person. For 4 people you would need 3 large peaches – if peaches are small use 1 per person. The hazelnut oil is especially good with this combination but, if this is unobtainable, try another nut oil.

Serves 4
3–4 peaches
a handful of fresh spinach leaves
a bunch of watercress
2 tablespoons toasted hazelnuts (see page 89), chopped

VINAIGRETTE
4 fl oz (125 ml) hazelnut oil
1 tablespoon best white wine vinegar
salt and pepper, to taste

Peel peaches, blanching them in hot water if necessary, halve, remove stones, slice, then chop into neat cubes. Mix vinaigrette ingredients together, pour over peaches and leave to marinate for 30 to 40 minutes. Wash and dry spinach leaves and watercress. Remove any tough stalks.

To serve, tear spinach leaves into pieces, place in a salad bowl and add watercress and peaches. Toss very gently, then sprinkle with toasted hazelnuts.

Peaches with Parma Ham

Peaches are even better with Parma ham than the traditional melon. Peel and slice the peaches and arrange on individual plates as you would melon.

Peach Soup

Lovely on a hot summer's day. This is a good recipe for using up the fruit before it is over-ripe but do use really ripe peaches.

Serves 6

8–10 peaches, depending on size

1 teaspoon grated orange peel

1/4–1/2 teaspoon curry paste or powder

6 fl oz (185 ml) plain yogurt

20 fl oz (625 ml) creamy milk or 10 fl oz (315 ml) milk and 10 fl oz (315 ml) cream

a tiny pinch of salt

1 tablespoon chopped fresh herbs, to finish (parsley, mint, coriander or chives are all good)

Peel the peaches. Slice in half lengthwise and remove stones. Place in a blender or food processor and purée, then add orange

peel, curry paste or powder and whizz again to mix. Next add yogurt, whizz again, then add creamy milk and salt. Mix well and leave to chill. Sprinkle with herbs just before serving.

Note: When using fresh peaches, do not forget that they will discolour, so work quickly and eat the same day as the soup is prepared.

The principall fruit trees which delight to be planted against a wall are peaches, abricots, nectaryas, all sorts of sweet plumbs.

(1616, Richard Surflet (trs) of C Estienne & J Liébault's 'Maison rustique or the countrie farme')

Grilled Peaches

Children love this dish and can cook it themselves (under supervision) on an outside barbecue. It is also good for using up unripe fruit.

1 peach each
1 teaspoon sweet chutney – mango is good
2 rashers bacon

Cut peaches in half and remove stones. Spread with chutney, place under a hot grill or on a barbecue and grill until chutney bubbles and begins to caramelize. Keep hot while you grill bacon rashers until crisp.

For grown-ups, try these peaches with grilled kidneys or gammon.

Peach & Chicken Salad

Peaches and curry complement each other well; this cold chicken dish uses both to excellent advantage in a summer salad.

For each person you will need about half a cup of cold cubed chicken and half a peach, peeled and chopped. And for the sauce, per person, mix together 2 teaspoons mayonnaise and 2 teaspoons plain yogurt, add a few drops of onion juice from a piece of onion squeezed through a garlic press and about ½ saltspoon, or to taste, of curry paste (paste is much better than powder if you are not cooking the curry powder in the usual way); salt and pepper and a heaped teaspoon of chopped fresh mint.

Fold the chicken and peach into this curry-flavoured sauce, pile into a dish and decorate with sprigs of fresh mint and slices of unpeeled peach.

Serve with a rice salad or new potatoes and a green salad.

No peachy marke to signifie distaine
No greene to shew a wanton mind and vaine.
(1599, Thomas Moufet 'Silkwormes and their
flies, lively described in verse')

Barbecued Peaches

For a delicious sweet version of the grilled peaches on page 54, fill the stone cavity with a mixture of butter, rum and sugar, which you have made by melting 1 oz (30 g) butter in a small pan and adding 1 tablespoon rum and 1 tablespoon caster sugar. Grill cut side up and serve hot, with whipped cream lightened with a teaspoon or two of thick Greek-style yogurt.

Peach Cake

To eat as a warm pudding. A good recipe for using up hard, unripe fruit.

Serves 8
4 oz (125 g) butter
4 oz (125 g) soft brown sugar
2 eggs
1 oz (30 g) ground almonds
1 oz (30 g) nibbed almonds
4 oz (125 g) self-raising flour
2–3 firm peaches, peeled and chopped
2–3 ripe peaches for filling and top
1 tablespoon Amaretto (almond) liqueur
6 fl oz (185 ml) double (heavy) cream, to serve

Butter well and line two 8 in (20 cm) cake tins. To make the cake, cream together butter and sugar in a bowl until light and fluffy. Add eggs one at a time, beating well in between, then add ground and nibbed almonds. Mix well, fold in flour and lastly

A wise man among monkeys and mice, intricately carved out of a peach stone ¾ in length

add chopped peaches. Turn into prepared cake tins and bake at 190 °C (375 °F/Gas 5) for 10 to 15 minutes, until deep golden and firm to touch in the middle. Turn out onto a wire rack and cool slightly.

While the cake is cooling, quickly peel and slice the ripe peaches, toss in the liqueur, then use to fill the centre of the cake and to pile on top.

Serve with a bowl of whipped cream. This cake should be served warm enough for the cream to melt while it is being eaten.

Peach
Stone

Peach Tart

This is a deep tart, so make the walls of your pastry as high as possible to allow room for the filling. Use the pastry recipe on page 87, which uses the melted butter method. Bake blind.

Serves 6–8

FILLING
3–4 peaches, peeled, halved and stoned
2 oz (60 g) butter
3 oz (90 g) caster sugar
3 eggs
3 oz (90 g) ground almonds
¼ oz (7 g) plain flour

Lay peach halves, cut side up, on pastry base. Cream butter and sugar together in a bowl until light and fluffy. Add eggs one by one, beating very well in between each egg. Fold in ground almonds and flour, pour over peach halves and bake at 190 °C (375 °F/Gas 5) for 20 to 25 minutes until pale golden and firm to the touch. This is best served warm.

Peach Tart II

Using the pastry base from the previous recipe and fresh ripe peaches, sliced and soaked in 1–2 tablespoons of a suitable liqueur or good brandy, you can make a delicious tart, which you must assemble at the last minute. Use the crème pâtissière recipe on page 88.

Serves 6–8

FILLING
about 8 fl oz (250 ml) crème pâtissière

3–4 ripe peaches or nectarines, peeled, sliced and soaked in 1–2 tablespoons liqueur or brandy

6 fl oz (185 ml) double (heavy) cream, whipped

toasted almonds, to decorate, if desired

To assemble the tart, first spread a layer of crème pâtissière on the pastry base, then arrange the liqueur-soaked peaches on top and finally spread a layer of whipped cream. Decorate with toasted almonds if liked.

Peach Cobbler

There are many versions of old-fashioned cobblers and many ways of making them. Eat this one piping hot with lots of thick cream to pour over.

Serves 4
4–5 peaches, depending on size
1–2 tablespoons dark rum
2–3 oz (60–90 g) caster sugar
1 oz (30 g) butter

TOPPING
4 oz (125 g) self-raising flour
2 oz (60 g) butter, cut in pieces
2 oz (60 g) caster sugar
1 egg
4 fl oz (125 ml) milk

Butter a 1½–2 pint (1–1.25 litre) ovenproof pie dish generously. Peel and slice peaches and place in the pie dish, sprinkle with rum and sugar, dot with butter. To make the topping, sieve flour into a mixing bowl and rub in butter until the mixture looks like breadcrumbs, then add sugar and mix well. Beat egg and milk together and pour into flour. Mix thoroughly and pour over peaches. If the batter seems too stiff, add a little milk. Bake at 190 °C (375 °F/Gas 5) for 20 to 30 minutes, until topping is set. Serve at once.

Peaches Fried in Brown Sugar & Rum

This is a quick and easy and very unusual dessert, which can be eaten hot or cold.

For each person allow at least 1 whole peach, peeled and sliced, 1 teaspoon butter, 2 teaspoons brown sugar and 1½ teaspoons dark rum.

Place all the ingredients in a large, clean frying pan and gently stir-fry until the sugar is dissolved, then add 2–3 teaspoons double (heavy) cream per person, bring to the boil and serve at once, or pour into a serving dish and chill.

Peaches in Cream

Serves 4–6
20 fl oz (625 ml) double (heavy) cream
1–2 teaspoons orange flower water
1–2 tablespoons caster sugar
4–5 ripe peaches, peeled and chopped
4 macaroons, roughly crushed

Place cream, orange flower water and sugar in a bowl and whip, taking care not to over-beat. Fold in peaches and chill for an hour before serving. Then, just before the delicious concoction is to be eaten, fold in macaroons.

Peaches Poached in Red Wine with Macaroons

A simple pudding after a rich meal. Peaches make a splendid addition to the famous Italian dessert of macaroons and red wine.

Serves 4
4 oz (125 g) sugar
20 fl oz (625 ml) water
4 ripe peaches
4 macaroons
*10–20 fl oz (315–625 ml) red wine –
not too rough*

Place sugar in a saucepan, add water and slowly bring to the boil, stirring until sugar is dissolved, then boil for 2 to 3 minutes. Peel and halve peaches and lay cut side up in a shallow flameproof dish. Pour over boiling syrup and leave to cool.

To serve, remove peaches from syrup and drain well on a wire rack for half an hour or pat dry with absorbent kitchen paper. Dip macaroons in red wine and sandwich between peach halves. Arrange in individual serving dishes, pour over enough red wine to serve as a juice – about 2–3 fl oz (60–90 ml) – and serve at once.

Note: The syrup can be reserved for use in other recipes. Store it in a covered jar in the fridge.

Peaches Poached with Elderflower

The beautifully-scented elderflowers impart a delicate flavour to peaches when poached together.

Serves 4

4 oz (125 g) sugar

25 fl oz (785 ml) water

4 complete elderflower heads, trimmed of their thick stalks

4 peaches, peeled and halved

Place sugar and water in a saucepan and make a syrup as described in the previous recipe. When sugar is dissolved, add elderflower heads – tied in muslin if you like – or else strain the syrup before adding the peaches. Boil very gently for 10 to 15 minutes, then remove elderflowers – or strain – and add peaches to syrup. Poach gently until just tender – the length of time depends on how ripe the peaches are. Chill and serve very cold.

Cheryes, strawberies, pesshes, medliers.
(1483, William Caxton 'Dialogue')

Stuffed Peaches

Serves 4

4 oz (125 g) sugar
20 fl oz (625 ml) water
4 ripe peaches, peeled and halved
2 oz (60 g) cake crumbs
1 oz (30 g) nibbed almonds
1/2 oz (15 g) ground almonds
2 tablespoons apricot jam
1–2 tablespoons white wine
8 toasted almonds
*1–2 tablespoons Amaretto (almond) or
other suitable liqueur*

Make a sugar syrup using the method in 'Peaches Poached in Red Wine' (see page 66). Pour syrup over peach halves and reserve. When cold, remove and drain but do not pat dry, reserving syrup. In a bowl mix together cake crumbs with almonds, jam and wine. Using a teaspoon, fill the cavities in the peaches with this stuffing. Top each peach with a toasted almond, place in a serving dish and pour round the syrup to which you have added 1–2 tablespoons of liqueur.

The downy peach, the shining plum,
The ruddy, fragrant nectarine.
(1730, James Thompson 'The Seasons:
Autumn')

Imogen's Frozen Peaches
A light and refreshing frozen pudding.

Serves 4–6
4 ripe peaches, peeled
1 lb (500 g) raspberries
6 oz (185 g) caster sugar
6 fl oz (185 ml) double (heavy) cream
1 egg white
2 tablespoons brandy

Blanch and peel peaches, slice thinly length-wise and place in a freezer tray or other suitable container. Reserving a few whole raspberries for decoration, place the rest in a blender or food processor with 4 oz (125 g) of the caster sugar and process to a purée. Whip cream, then whip egg white in a separate bowl. Slowly beating in remaining sugar, fold cream into raspberry purée. Fold in egg white and pour or spoon over sliced peaches. Freeze for 2 to 3 hours or until firm.

To serve, remove from the freezer and leave at room temperature for 10 minutes, then turn out and decorate with reserved raspberries.

A gray velvet bodice that fitted the plump, supple figure, as the rind fits the peach.
(1884, Miss Mary E Braddon 'Ishmael')

Whole Peaches in Rum

A great extravagance, but worth it!

Take a large, wide-necked jar and pack it with layers of peeled peaches and sugar. When the jar is tightly packed and filled to the brim top up with dark rum. Put a plate or saucer on top and a weight to keep the fruit submerged, and cover with a lid, plastic wrap or foil. Leave for at least three months.

Peach Curd

More of a pudding or cake filling than a spread for bread. To serve as a pudding, try it as a base for sliced peaches or strawberries or eat with sponge fingers. Thinned with a little white wine, it makes a good sauce to pour over ice cream.

Makes 3–4 small jars

10 fl oz (315 ml) peach purée, see 'Apricot Purée' recipe on page 36

4 oz (125 g) sugar

4 oz (125 g) unsalted butter

5 egg yolks, beaten

few drops pure vanilla extract or 1 tablespoon Amaretto (almond) liqueur or good brandy

Place peach purée in a double boiler, add sugar and butter and stir over a gentle heat until sugar and butter are dissolved. Add egg yolks and stir until the mixture has thickened. Stir in vanilla extract or liqueur. Pour into clean, warm jars, cover (see page 88) and store in the refrigerator.

A delicate peachy bloom of complexion, very common in England.

> *(1755, Barry 'Obstruct Arts Eng')*

Peach & Curry Sauce or Relish

This is a sauce you can make in a double quantity and store in the fridge or even freeze. It goes well with pork and chicken or quail or partridge. It is also suitable for nectarines and apricots.

1 tablespoon cooking oil
1 small onion, chopped
1 teaspoon curry paste or powder, or to taste
3 tablespoons cider vinegar
10 fl oz (315 ml) cider
4–5 peaches, peeled and chopped
salt and pepper, to taste
1–2 teaspoons sugar, if desired

Heat oil in a saucepan, add onion and fry gently for 5 minutes, do not brown, then add curry paste or powder and cook for 1 minute. Stir in vinegar and bring to the boil, then add cider and chopped peaches, cover and simmer for 20 to 30 minutes. Add salt and pepper. Taste for flavour and, if it appears a bit weak, boil down and reduce the liquor. Otherwise, tip into a blender or food processor and purée until smooth. Taste again and adjust seasoning; at this stage you may like to add a teaspoon or two of sugar.

To store, pour into a clean container, cover and refrigerate.

Peches doeth mollyfy the bely, and be colde.
(1542, Andrew Boorde 'A compendius regyment
or a dyetary of helth')

Peach Chutney

A mild chutney, or relish, too delicate for a true chutney and all the nicer for it.

Makes about 3 jars
2 lb (1 kg) peaches, prepared weight
1/2 an onion, finely chopped
8 fl oz (250 ml) cider
2 in (5 cm) stick cinnamon
4 whole allspice
4 fl oz (125 ml) cider vinegar
8 oz (250 g) soft brown sugar

Peel, stone, chop and weigh peaches. Place in a large saucepan with onion, cider and spices, bring to the boil and simmer gently, stirring all the time, for 15 to 20 minutes, until fruit is cooked. Add vinegar and sugar and boil for a further 45 minutes, until the mixture is dark and thickening. Remove from the heat, cool slightly, pot and cover (see page 88). Store in a cool, dry place. Keep at least one month before using, then, once opened, store in the fridge.

The velvet Peach, gilt Orange, downy Quince.
(1591, Sylvester 'Du Bartas his divine weekes
and workes')

Spiced Peaches

This is rather a sweet, mellow syrup but
better, I think, than a vinegary concoction.
Serve with cold meats.

Makes 2–3 jars
5 fl oz (155 ml) cider vinegar
10 fl oz (315 ml) cider
1 lb (500 g) sugar
2 in (5 cm) stick cinnamon
4 whole allspice
8 peppercorns
1 bay leaf
2 lb (1 kg) peaches, peeled and halved

Place cider vinegar, cider and sugar in a
saucepan and heat gently until sugar has dissolved. Add spices and bay leaf and simmer
for 5 to 7 minutes. Add peach halves – do not
overcrowd – and poach very carefully until
just tender; cooking time depends on the
ripeness of the fruit. Using a slotted spoon,
remove fruit and pack into clean, warm jars.
Strain the juice and pour over fruit. Cover
and store in a cool, dry place. Leave for at
least a month before using.

NECTARINES

This smooth, plum-skinned variety of the peach with its red-tinged skin and flesh has a sharper taste and stronger scent and flavour than many varieties of peach. Most of the peach recipes given are equally suitable for nectarines. There are, though, a few recipes where nectarines, with their sharpness, are superior to peaches. 'Nectarine Dream' would be rather too sweet if peaches were substituted and a 'Nectarine Bavarois', if made with peaches, could be too bland.

Nectarine Dream

Serves 4
8 nectarines
1 1/2 oz (45 g) butter
2 tablespoons brown sugar
4 fl oz (125 ml) double (heavy) cream
4 macaroons
2 tablespoons Amaretto (almond) liqueur

Peel, stone and slice nectarines. Melt butter in a pan over a low heat, then add brown sugar and nectarines. Gently stir-fry for 3 to 5 minutes, then pour on cream and mix well. Pour into a dish and leave to cool. Just before serving, break macaroons into bite-sized pieces, fold into nectarines and sprinkle with Amaretto.

Nectarine Bavarois

This delectable dessert can be made using the recipe for fully poached fruit as given in 'Peaches Poached with Elderflower', page 67. If the nectarines are very ripe use the method for 'Peaches Poached in Red Wine' on page 66.

Serves 4–6

*1 lb (500 g) prepared weight nectarines –
about 4–5 large fruits*

2 oz (60 g) sugar, or to taste

1/2 oz (15 g) powdered gelatine

4 tablespoons hot water

1 tablespoon orange flower water

*8 fl oz (250 ml) double (heavy) or
whipping cream*

few slices of nectarine, to serve

Poach fruit according to the chosen method. While still hot, remove from juice and purée

80

in a blender or food processor, then add sugar. In a small bowl or cup, sprinkle gelatine over hot water, mix and add to the hot purée. Stir until gelatine is dissolved, then leave to cool. When quite cool and starting to set round the edges, beat well and add orange flower water. In another bowl whip cream and fold into nectarine mixture. Rinse a 2 pint (1.2 litre) mould with cold water, pour in the bavarois and leave to set.

To serve, turn out onto a pretty serving dish and decorate with a few slices of ripe nectarine.

I shall joyne the Nectrine with the Aprecock although another kind of fruit.
  (1657, Ralph Austen 'Treatise on fruit trees')

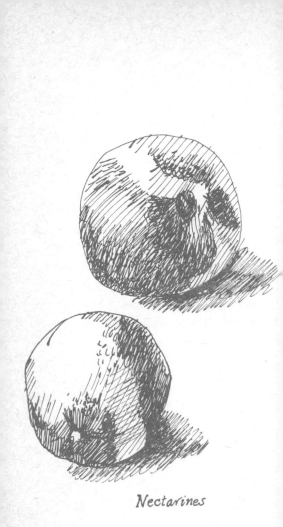

Nectarines

Fresh Nectarine Dessert

This is exquisite when made with really fine, ripe fruit; white peaches are equally good. This is, however, a last minute dish.

For six to eight people you will need 1 whole peach each plus 4–5 nectarines to make a purée with. Blanch all the peaches in boiling water, then skin, halve and remove stones. Chop 4 or 5 nectarines and place in a blender or food processor and purée, add 2–3 tablespoons good brandy and 2–3 tablespoons caster sugar; purée again. Place the peach halves in a serving dish and pour over the purée, serve at once. Hand round a plate of ratafias, small macaroons or other almond biscuits. If you like the fruit chilled, keep in the refrigerator for 4 to 6 hours before using.

Black eyes, nectarine bloom and pouting rosy lips.
(1854, Marion Harland 'Alone')

*Nectarine
stone*

Nectarine Ice Cream

Serves 6–8

*1 lb (500 g) nectarines, weighed after
peeling and stoning*

2 eggs, separated

6 oz (185 g) caster sugar

*20 fl oz (625 ml) double (heavy) cream,
whipped*

2 tablespoons brandy, if desired

Chop nectarines and purée in a blender or
food processor. Whip egg yolks with half the
sugar. Whip egg whites in another bowl until
stiff, then add remaining sugar a little at a
time, beating well in between. Whip cream
with brandy in a third bowl. Now add nectarines to egg yolks and fold into cream. Lastly
fold in stiffly-beaten egg whites. Turn into a
2½ pint (1.5 litre) freezer container and
freeze until firm.

Nectarine Sorbet

Serves 4–6

*20 fl oz (625 ml) nectarine purée, see
'Apricot Purée', page 36*

2 oz (60 g) icing sugar

juice of 1 orange

1 egg white

2 oz (60 g) caster sugar

Mix together nectarine purée, icing sugar and orange juice; pour into a 2 pint (1.2 litre) freezer container and freeze for 2 to 3 hours. Remove from the freezer and break up to a mush. Whip egg white until stiff, then add caster sugar a little at a time, beating well in between. Fold into nectarine mixture and return to the freezer until firm. Transfer to the refrigerator to soften a little 15 to 20 minutes before serving.

Nectarine Nectar
Serves 2–3

To 10 fl oz (315 ml) purée (see 'Apricot Purée', page 36), add 5 fl oz (155 ml) thick plain yogurt and 5 fl oz (155 ml) creamy milk. Whizz in a blender or food processor. Place a scoop of vanilla ice cream in a tall glass and pour over the nectar.

Nectarine

BASICS

Pastry Base

This pastry recipe will fill a 9 in (22.5 cm) flan tin or an 8 in (20 cm) deep tart tin.

2 oz (60 g) butter
2 oz (60 g) sugar
4 oz (125 g) plain flour, sieved

Melt butter very slowly in a saucepan, do not allow it to get too hot. Stir in sugar, remove from the heat and leave to cool slightly, then stir in flour. Mix well together, then press firmly into base and up the side of the tin.

Bake blind in a moderately hot oven, 200 °C (400 °F/Gas 6) for 15 minutes until pale golden.

Crème Pâtissière

1 heaped teaspoon cornflour
5 fl oz (155 ml) milk
2 oz (60 g) sugar
2 egg yolks, beaten
4 oz (125 g) unsalted butter
vanilla extract, to taste

Blend cornflour with milk in a bowl until smooth, then pour into a saucepan. Add sugar and egg yolks and cook gently over a low heat, stirring all the time, until the mixture thickens and becomes smooth. Bring just to the boil to cook the cornflour then remove from the heat and beat hard. Leave to cool, stirring occasionally. When almost cold, beat in butter, a knob at a time, then beat in vanilla and leave to cool completely.

To Pot Jam, Curd or Preserves

Potting must be done correctly to keep food from developing bacteria.

Make sure that the jars are completely sterile, warm and dry. Remove any foam that may have formed on the surface of the jam and pot carefully and quickly. Fill jars to the brim, cover with wax circles, then seal with self-sealing lids. Label and store in a cool, dark place or the fridge, as directed.

To Toast Hazelnuts Easily

Heat a dry, clean frying pan, pour in the nuts and 'toast' dry over the heat. When the nuts are dark brown all over, tip into a sieve and rub off the skins. Do not chop until cold. You can prepare more of these than you require as they will keep for 4 to 6 weeks if stored in a screw-topped jar in a dry place.

Freezing

Apricots, peaches and nectarines all freeze well. Apricots can be frozen without peeling. Choose ripe, unblemished fruit, halve and remove stone. Peaches and nectarines should be blanched, peeled and sliced. To prevent discoloration, dip in a solution of juice of 1 lemon to 20 fl oz (625 ml) water, then pack tightly in plastic freezer boxes layered with sugar, using 4–6 oz (125–185 g) to every 1 lb (500 g) of fruit.

All are excellent frozen in a sugar syrup, made using 6–8 oz (185–250 g) sugar to 20 fl oz (625 ml) water. Dissolve over a slow heat, bring to the boil, cool and pour over the fruit: 6 fl oz (185 ml) should cover 1 lb (500 g) apricots or sliced peaches or nectarines. Pack in plastic containers.

These fruit freeze equally well in purée form. To every 20 fl oz (625 ml) purée, add 6 oz (185 g) caster sugar, mix well, pack at once in plastic containers and cover tightly.

INDEX